For my friends when relaxing

Acknowledgements

Thanks to the editors of *Critical Survey*, who published 'The Progress of Life' and 'The Progress of Art'.
Cover Photo: Gary Walsh.

Previous collections by Richard Kell

Fantasy Poets (pamphlet, Oxford 1957)
Control Tower (1962)
Differences (1969)
Humours (1978)
Heartwood (pamphlet, 1978)
The Broken Circle (1981)
In Praise of Warmth: New & Selected (1987)
Rock and Water (1993)
Collected Poems (2001)
Under the Rainbow (2003)
Letters to Enid (2004)

TAKING A BREAK

A lot of limericks

RICHARD KELL

Shoestring Press

Typeset and Printed by Parker and Collinson Ltd.
Nottingham NG7 2FH
(0115) 942 0140

Published by Shoestring Press
19 Devonshire Avenue, Beeston, Nottingham, NG9 1BS
(0115) 925 1827
www.shoestringpress.co.uk

First Published 2008

ISBN: 978 1 904886 80 8

Shoestring Press gratefully acknowledges financial assistance from Arts Council England.

FOREWORD

Before keyboards began to take over from pens, some serious authors doodled, wistfully or wickedly or both, in the margins of their rough drafts. One of my own ways of seeking relief from the pressures of engaged writing has been to compose limericks now and then. Hence the following collection, which I hope those who enjoy carefully shaped verse of every sort will find refreshing. Such dedicated readers are offered here a temporary release from political and moral correctness, perhaps something like the licence allowed during the medieval Feast of Fools.

In making the collection I have sorted a jumble as far as possible. So a defiantly mixed bunch of limericks (1-53) is followed by ones about religion (54-71), sex (72-82), art (83-86), natural and human history (87-112) and finally, in plain lyrical mode (an experiment dear to my heart), common scenes and experiences (113-130). Along the way there are a few funny-serious argumentative 'poems' with limerick stanzas, and to these I have given titles. I offer also an Afterword in the form of an extended limerick.

R.K.
2007

1 Seeing Tanka and Limerick fighting,
Jim said 'Why not both kinds of writing?'
They stopped and they stared,
Then they cordially paired
To give that intruder a smiting.

2 A marvellous magician called Betty
Plunged into the sea from a jetty.
She sped through a maze
Of underworld ways,
Then popped up in front of the Yeti.

3 Here's the photo: 'Mysterious Blonde'.
As I mentioned, she lives in the pond.
You can see that I've caught her
Half out of the water
And holding what looks like a wand.

4 A sorcerer mad about beer
Put an end to a dazzling career
When, hopelessly fuddled,
He got a spell muddled
And made his own head disappear.

5 An endearing bohemian actor
Went around on a secondhand tractor.
It still isn't clear
Why he drove off a pier
But being drunk was a probable factor.

6 Big drinker and eater, old Artie
Was also the soul of the party -
Until, halfway through,
He was ripe for the loo
And became unapproachably farty.

7 The landlady said to the louse,
'Now why have you come to my house?'
To which it replied
'I was taking a ride
On an intimate part of your spouse.'

8 A dreamy young woman called Janet
Was longing to fly like a gannet.
She tried an as-if
From the top of a cliff,
And now she has gone from our planet.

9 Said a clever young fellow in Goa,
On being released by a boa,
'I thwarted a feast
By informing the beast
I'm a reincarnation of Noah.'

10 A voluble pedant from Italy,
Whose lips were excessively spittle-y,
Displayed mental power
With the help of a shower
When passing on rules jot-and-tittle-y.

11 A hopeful young tenor from Guinea
Had a voice people told him was tinny.
    He went to a coach
    With a novel approach
And now he's being told not to whinny.

12 A friendly young man from Peru
Went every weekend to the zoo.
    'The thing I like best,'
    He shyly confessed,
'Is the elephant doing its poo.'

13 Imagine pipe-smoking Priscilla
Installed in a grotty old villa -
    Alone but not quite,
    Because, every night,
She cuddles an orphaned gorilla.

14 Maisie Madison, fresh from Versailles,
Exclaimed on the phone 'Mailles oh mailles!
    Such elegant chairs
    And magnificent stairs
And you've never seen ceilings so hailles!'

15 I remarked to a friend near Marseille,
'It's a good deille for meilleking the heille.'
    He scowled and said 'Surely',
    Then added obscurely
'But Adam was meilled out of cleille.'

16* Re electrons, Prince Louis de Broglie
Said 'The moment has come to emploglie
My theory of waves,
Put an end to the raves
That the particle mongers enjoglie.'

17 The grandson of Henri de Broglie
Was given a delicate toglie.
He hurled it with glee
At the trunk of a tree
And his nanny exclaimed 'Wicked boglie!'

18 A versatile actress called Niamh
Said that what she'd most like to achiamh
Was a powerful portrayal
Of pride and betrayal
As first represented by Iamh.

19 Last autumn the people of Bern
Were deeply astonished to learn
That a number of scalps
Had been found in the Alps
With a tomahawk, firestick and urn.

20 A uranium scout, probing Eiger,
Encountered, of all things, a tiger.
Though sceptics may sneer,
We recovered his gear
And his bones with the help of Herr Geiger.

* The French pronunciation of Broglie is approximately *broy*. Actually de Broglie showed in 1924 that electrons can be both waves and particles.

21 Some speak of the music as jazzy,
And all are agreed that it's snazzy.
  Well written or not
  It's undoubtedly hot
And infuriates Prince Esterhazy.

22 I hear with amazement that Bruce,
Once a rip, has become a recluse.
  He lives in an attic,
  His thoughts are Socratic,
And now he drinks nothing but juice.

23 Diogenes-like, little Greg
Stole away and moved into a keg.
  But he went back to Mum
  When his deep-thinking tum
Argued strongly for bacon and egg.

24 When excited, a mate on a schooner
Got muddled like poor Doctor Spooner.
  His cries - 'Whet the gale!
  Ban the moats!' - couldn't fail
To confuse any newcome harpooner.

25 The spire on the Seal Trainers Hall,
As firm and as sharp as an awl,
  Was reported one night
  (The observers weren't tight)
To be wobbling and flicking a ball.

26 The riverside residents laughed
At a fellow who lived on a raft.
    But when hit by a flood
    Filling houses with mud
They envied that floater his craft.

27 A Wimbledon prodigy, Ewing
Has many an acolyte stewing.
    Enchanted by Venice
    He's given up tennis
And taken to solo canoeing.

28 'We're unlike,' replied Breakfast to Dinner,
When the action of both became inner,
    'Not in kind but degree:
    You're exactly like me
Only fatter - or, sorry, I'm thinner.'

29 When a crocodile met a canoe,
He said 'I don't think much of you.'
    But he then heard a shout,
    Got a whack on the snout,
And rapidly altered his view.

30 Said a zebra who met a giraffe,
'Your neck should be shortened by half.
    Your markings are fine
    Though unequal to mine
But your brainbox is right off the graph.'

31 A precocious young lady in Cork
Was told she'd been brought by the Stork.
    This she firmly denied,
    Insisting with pride
She'd been placed on a beach by the Orc.

32 The weather's at ninety degrees.
That seems not to bother the bees,
    But I'm hot in the head
    So I'll dream up a sled
And a sea that still knows how to freeze.

33 It's a *Wish You Were Here* from Dan Cole:
'Enjoying my adventurous role.
    We were flown to the spot
    Reached by A before Scott.
Lots of ice but no sign of the pole.'

34 When asked why he lived in a tent,
Bing Blicester, a funny old gent,
    Explained 'Well, a house
    Isn't much for a mouse',
But nobody knew what he meant.

35 Archie emails 'I bathe in the river,
Though in winter the cold makes me shiver!
    I'm frightfully keen
    On this daily routine
Because Aunt says it's good for my liver.'

36 Why a manic young poet called Russ
Lost his day job of driving a bus
Was that, metaphor-popping,
He drove without stopping,
Ignoring both red lights and us.

37 A dignified lady called Alice
Drank tea from a fine silver chalice.
She liked eating venison,
Reading Lord Tennyson
And listening to music by Tallis.

38 'I,' boasted ghost-hunter Magee,
'Frighten them more than they frighten me.
I blow a brief tune
On my double-bassoon,
From which they unfailingly flee.'

39 When Cliff tried to learn the trombone,
He produced little more than a moan.
But he said 'When I die
I shall practise on high
Till I'm playing at the heavenly throne.'

40 Though pretty and passionate, Ella
Has never attracted a fella.
You want to know why?
Well, she's terribly shy
So she hides underneath an umbrella.

41 Until he turned forty, our Dave
Was quiet and careful and grave.
But then he met Mo,
Who said 'Learn to let go',
And now his whole life is a rave.

42 After handyman Chris cut the hedge,
We were shocked by its raggedy edge.
But in future, we hope,
He'll be able to cope,
Having recently taken the pledge.

43 Though exceedingly lovable, Suzy
Was as indolent as she was boozy.
All day she'd recline,
While sipping her wine,
On a sofa or in the jacuzzi.

44 The author, who lived in Tobruk,
Was blurbed as a wonderful cook.
The book, though a winner,
Spoiled many a dinner,
That whizz being a versatile crook.

45 No better deceiver than Frank!
He gambled, whored, swindled and drank;
But doing these discreetly
He managed life neatly
And rose to the top in a bank.

46 Roberto, once mad about yachting,
Went madder and took to garrotting.
Caught using a saw,
Then 'garrotted' by law,
He's now buried and peacefully rotting.

47 'Now which do you reckon's more shitty,
The life of a village or city?'
He says 'It depends - '
But the answer offends
And she tells him his thinking is bitty.

48 When a jetliner captain went manic
(The co-pilot's word was 'satanic'),
His looping the loop
Made the passengers whoop,
Not with joy but in absolute panic.

49 'You should never say thankyou or sorry'
Was a maxim arrived at by Florry.
Her husband said both,
Then added an oath,
When he tumbled her into a quarry.

50 When I pondered the missiles of NATO
Along with the teachings of Plato,
My tutor said 'Pat,
You're not ready for that.
Let's consider the humble potato.'

51 Several others will soon know what I know:
Poor Jekyll's becoming a wino.
He was found after dark
In a lane near the park
Shrieking 'Why have I changed to a rhino?'

52 A don in his prime went to bed
And stayed there until he was dead.
'How long?' you may ask.
Well, he finished the task
Of blanking out all he had read.

53 A promiscuous fellow, young Barry
Was urged by his mother to marry.
He did, but went on
In the way he had gone,
Vexing her and delighting Old Harry.

54 Appealed to by Moody and Sankey,
A sinner responded 'I thank ee.
But pardon me, gents,
Your holy events
Ain't a patch on the old hanky-panky.'

55 A Papist confessed to a Prod,
'I'm sometimes confused about God.
It's a bit of a tease
That such different peas
Should have come from the very same pod.'

56 A smooth charismatic divine
Had a secret addiction to wine.
  It didn't much aid
  His belief when he prayed
But it certainly helped him to shine.

57 What sinners confess to the priest
Will never go further. At least
  I believed it was so
  Till a cleric I know
Drank too much at a funeral feast.

58 When a cardinal said to the Pope,
'Maybe alms should include lots of soap',
  His Holiness sighed
  And archly replied,
'To wash away sinspots I hope.'

59 In Pit Ninety a serious row,
All torture suspended for now:
  Two archfiends disputing,
  Mid cheering and hooting,
The claim to Unholier Than Thou.

60-66 **The Problem of Evil**

Said Adam, convicted of sin,
'We humans can't possibly win.
  If not within God,
  Since I'm made from a clod,
Where did evil intentions begin?'

An avuncular seraph replied,
'They started in Lucifer's pride,
    A failing passed on,
    Where the apple tree shone,
To you and your beautiful bride.'

Then Adam: 'If God fashioned all,
From seraphs to creatures that crawl,
    He must have built in
    What made Lucifer sin:
He himself therefore triggered the Fall.'

Said the seraph 'That's not how it ran.
What he gave to both angels and man
    Was freedom of will
    To embrace good or ill:
He didn't want simply to ban.'

'So,' said A, 'he created us free
Yet forbade us the fruit of the tree,
    Then got all irate
    When we chose and we ate:
That seems a bit batty to me.

'Where only one choice is allowed,
What's the freedom with which we're endowed?
    "They scorned Yahweh's gift"
    Is the scholarly drift
But to my mind it's Yahweh who's proud.

'Even choosing the good or the ill
Is a notion that baffles me still.
    If the whole world was good
    Like its maker, how *could*
Any evil have tugged at the will?'

67 Forgive me: that's more than enough
Of my deep theological stuff.
It's time to relax,
Turn from organ to sax,
Get back to the earthy and bluff.

68 The world is wet, windy and dark,
Huge billows are bashing the Ark,
And Noah, now queasy
As well as uneasy,
Is growling 'How's this for a lark.'

69 When all were afloat in the Ark,
A lookout dog started to bark.
In reply to 'What is it?'
He shouted 'A visit!
What grub can we give to a shark?'

70 Jehovah, on spotting the Ark,
Called out to his chronicle clerk,
'It's them, come and look!
This is one for the Book!
They're certainly making their mark!'

71 'Please pass me a drachma' said Zeus.
'I need an objective excuse.
It's essential to spin
Since I like a clear win
And a draw is all prayers can produce.'

72 Siobhan was a little bit fat,
But no less attractive for that.
    In fact she could stun
    When she lounged in the sun
Wearing only a smile and a hat.

73 I once knew a woman called Jane
Who loved walking nude in the rain.
    Male neighbours were glad
    When the weather turned bad,
But females were apt to complain.

74 A glamorous gal in Kentucky
Was thought by the guys to be fucky.
    But when one of them said
    'Will you join me in bed?'
She slapped him and cried 'Don't be mucky!'

75 The weather of marriage to Milly
Swung daily from sultry to chilly.
    She held in disdain
    Basil's very small brain
But was thrilled by his very big willy.

76 A Glaswegian, familiarly 'Jock',
Took pride in the length of his cock.
    When lovely Elaine
    Spoke of size with disdain,
He never got over the shock.

77 A corner-shop owner called Marge
Had breasts that were pleasingly large.
If a bloke bought enough
Of her regular stuff
She'd reveal them without extra charge.

78 Said a lass on the isle of Wakiti,
'I like my young men to be meaty.'
When a sailor said 'Ducky,
You mean fucky-fucky?'
She said 'No, I mean eaty-eaty.'

79 An inquisitive youngster called Danny
Once peeped at his going-to-bed nanny.
He found that where he
Had Sir Willywink, she
Had a part he would learn to call Fanny.

80 A sex queen (her stage name was Heather)
Looked stunning in satin or leather.
But quite a few men
Were much happier when
She appeared wearing only a feather.

81 A stripper now well up the ladder,
Melissa gets madder and madder.
I've heard on the street
That a forthcoming treat
Is a devilish fling with an adder.

82 Of Bob, who is brilliant at rugger,
It's whispered he's also a bugger.
His allies declare
The suspicion's unfair,
That he's gayish but only a hugger.

83-86* **The Progress of Art**

Should our shortlist for ultimate phoney
Include the late Piero Manzoni?
A canful of shit
May be something like wit
But as art it is utter boloney.

Some say my opinion's absurd.
They zap it with 'What's in a word?
The spirit of art
Being matched by a fart,
Its embodiment's matched by a turd.'

Others sketch a more colourful plot:
'There was magic at work in the pot.
Pure genius informed
What a body had warmed
And made it commercially hot.'

Ah Piero, how generous of you
To have passed on your artified poo.
But a few of us think,
Though you spared us the stink,
That it should have been piped from the loo.

* Piero Manzoni (1933-63) sold cans of his own faeces labelled 'Merda d'Artista'. Any one of them, I read, is now worth a small fortune.

87 Life's a wonder, a blessing, a shame,
An adventure, a nightmare, a game…
But the gene says it's feeding
And mating and breeding
To bring about more of the same.

88 Life draws on the sun and the rain,
But what it does then is insane.
No psalmist could sweeten
Its 'Eat and be eaten':
The logic alone is a pain.

89* An archaean enquired 'Who's the joker
That made us inhabit a smoker?'
The spirit addressed,
Who'd come up for a rest,
Said 'Search me, mate, I'm only a stoker.'

90 'Is heaven above, hell below?'
Said a thoughtful archaean. 'If so,
Surely we were designed,
Being a smokerish kind,
Not by God but his mischievous foe.'

91 At a vent in the bed of the ocean,
A microbe exclaimed 'What a notion!
Some creature called Man
Is convinced he began
Like ourselves but got godly promotion.'

* *archaean*: micro-organism broadly similar to a bacterium.
smoker: hot spring from deep-ocean volcanic vent.

92-96 **The Progress of Life**

Now why did the first protozoon,
With little but acid to go on,
Do something that led
To the conjugal bed,
Then to princes and prelates and so on?

Were the ultimate founders of nations
Wee copying kits and mutations,
Or did some design,
As our pontiffs opine,
Foreshadow the grand generations?

What a history, plan or no plan,
That primordial fission began!
A competitive 'will'
To survive, breed and kill
Journeyed on in the measures of Man.

I see ologies, cracies and isms,
Establishments, dogmas and schisms,
The triumph of greed
Over millions in need,
And flaws in utopian prisms.

Am I flummoxed and floundering? Yes.
I'm a kind of agnostic I guess:
Not a no-one-can-know one
But a which-way-to-go one
Whose mind's in a terrible mess.

97 Said Mike, 'Being cousins to chimps,
No wonder we're troubled by imps.
But I'm glad that our race
Has that simian trace:
Without it we might have been wimps.'

98 With his arrows, Attila the Hun
Had plenty of slaughterous fun -
    And could not have had more,
    Were it measured in gore,
If he'd picked off his foes with a gun.

99 'This bloodshed,' quoth Erik the Viking,
'I find very much to my liking.
    No man can be bored
    Who has axe, dirk and sword
To ensure lots of hacking and spiking.'

100 When the champions of Christendom prayed,
And a priest cried 'God bless our Crusade',
    Jehovah felt proud
    Seeing manly heads bowed
And foreknowing the work of the blade.

101-106* **Memetic Competition at a Party**

A Polking declared to a Dawk,
'You have little more soul than an auk.
    It's perfectly plain
    You're abusing your brain
And I'm tired of your arrogant squawk.'

The other replied with a laugh,
'Like old Johnny you're stiff as a staff!
    You too wear the collar
    And sound like a scholar
But couldn't outwit a giraffe.'

'Richard's notions,' the Polking retorted,
'Now yours, had been better aborted.
    His logic's astute
    Therefore hard to refute
But his vision is badly distorted.'

And so they'd go on, head to head,
While people like me were in bed.
    Each in turn would rehearse,
    With his blessing or curse,
What some dean or Darwinian said.

One guest, a nonpartisan friend,
Wide awake and amused to the end,
    Reports that by dawn
    They were out on the lawn
And that neither was willing to bend.

By ten, each was wielding a tome
And assaulting his enemy's dome.
    But a little while after,
    With tears and with laughter,
They warmly embraced and went home.

* In *The Selfish Gene* Richard Dawkins posits competition among memes as among genes. In *The God Delusion* he knocks the physicist and clergyman John Polkinghorne.

107 If selection is working on memes,
Has it meddled with mythical themes?
I hope it can't rule
The deep archetype pool,
Conditioning even my dreams.

108-112 **The Nature of Humanity**

'What's life, on the plane of zoology,
If not an outrageous tautology?'
To this, cousin Hugh
Adds '*We're* animals too,
And love is no more than biology.'

I find myself warmly concurring,
Then, wobbly as ever, demurring.
I mention the cat,
When she's brought in a rat,
Devotedly rubbing and purring.

A predator sprouting a soul?
Then I speak of her motherly role:
With affectionate tongue
She will comfort her young,
With wisdom direct and control.

Hugh scoffs 'What a barrel of shite!
Kittens turn into prowlers that bite -
And kids who have come
From a mafia mum
Get wise to the truth Might Is Right.'

Well, Hugh is more forceful than me,
So it's difficult not to agree.
Yet I like to believe,
Though he thinks me naïve,
There's true love in our family tree.

113 Don't tell me the limerick's wrong
For a charming description or song.
    Between popular rhyme
    And poetic sublime
There's no break though the pathway is long.

114 A bright little girl in Beijing
Is encouraged to dance and to sing.
    She has joy when it's light,
    Sweet dreams in the night,
And a name that means 'bird on the wing'.

115 Rich blossoms, unthreatening skies,
The fragrance, the birdsong! Our eyes
    And nostrils and ears
    Wake a love that inheres
In the spirit of Homo the Wise.

116 Some nights there was jazz with the beer.
We gladly stopped yakking to hear
    Those tunes and that beat,
    Chords pungent or sweet,
And breaks that we wanted to cheer.

117 Young families are playing on the green.
At the pond, with its fountain-flicked sheen,
    A little boy chucks
    Bits of bread to the ducks
And his dad is camcording the scene.

118 A rock pool unruffled and clear;
Two hunkering toddlers who peer
Among fronds for a glimpse
Of starfish or shrimps
While their mothers are watchfully near.

119 Miles away from a cove or a dock,
A beam circles high over rock.
Making dark water glint
With its silvery print,
It flashes as true as a clock.

120 There's a tree-shaded cleft in a hill
Where I loved watching clear water spill.
Its pools and cascades
And shiny glissades
(With glissandos) are haunting me still.

121 The freeze they must live with today
Has ended their snowballing play.
But now they can glide
On a supersmooth slide,
And shoes make more vibes than a sleigh!

122 Kids dashing around on the mud,
Shrill voices and toe-to-ball thud:
Worldwide it's the same,
The 'beautiful game'
And maybe a hero in bud.

123 When another week's work has been done,
People come to the river for fun.
    Its calm water shimmers
    While swans, boats and swimmers
Are sharing the afternoon sun.

124 Whizz-bang-crackle! Such fulminous flowers!
Burst rainbows' fountainy showers!
    Their magical light
    Fills the river tonight
And we're sensing primordial powers.

125 It was one of their Sunday delights
To be out in the wind with their kites.
    Humble fabric on string
    Then seemed to take wing
For rapturous heavenly flights.

126 Here's a schoolboy enchanted by rain
On the pathway, the leaves and the pane.
    He loves puddly plops
    Made by pellety drops
Scoring bullseyes again and again.

127 That balance, that disciplined ease -
And the snow-spray, the hiss of the skis,
    A backdrop alight
    In the sun, purest white -
As they skim toward chalets and trees.

128 There's a glimmer of dawn on the lake,
And a sigh where the bulrushes shake.
  Someone raps on the door
  Of a house by the shore,
But only the watchdog's awake.

129 'Never meddle with matches' they said,
So he didn't. But watching instead,
  He thought how the flame
  And the wood were the same
Until something alive became dead.

130 'Put the shell to your ear' said Marie.
'What you'll hear is the voice of the sea.'
  When I listened, I found
  That the whispery sound
Seemed a curious echo of me.

AFTERWORD

Most lovers of humour revere
The memories of Dodgson and Lear,
    And those who write verse
    Entertainingly terse -
Or endeavour to write it, as here -
    Know that metre with rhyme,
    Whether low or sublime,
Is an art. You're mistaken, my dear
    (That's 'dear reader' in short),
    If you think this is sport:
Well it is and it isn't, that's clear.
    There's simply no way
    This ostensible play,
Even boosted by whisky or beer,
    Could have helped me to slip
    From a classical grip
By excluding the wise and austere.
    The fact is I've tried
    Very hard to decide
Whether word-choices clash or cohere,
    No less in these pages
    Than those (quoting sages)
I've toiled at for over a year.
    So how can I plead
    That that brain-racking screed
Is more true to my nature? I fear
    That I won't find relief
    In the jokey and brief,
The anti-Miltonic, the mere:
    Though lighter of touch
    It involves me as much
As the stuff that is rather severe.
    In a nutshell, my heart
    Seems devoted to art,

Or craft if you will. Folk who sneer
    At nonsensical writing
    Deserve a good flyting
If only from heaven by Lear,
    Who must find it a pleasure
    That millions now treasure
The form that so tickled his ear.